Other titles in the UWAP Poetry series (established 2016)

Our Lady of the Fence Post by J. H. Crone

Border Security by Bruce Dawe

Melbourne Journal by Alan Loney

Star Struck by David McCooey

Dark Convicts by Judy Johnson

Rallying by Quinn Eades

Flute of Milk by Susan Fealy

A Personal History of Vision by Luke Fischer

Snake Like Charms by Amanda Joy

Charlie Twirl by Alan Gould

Afloat in Light by David Adès

Communists Like Us by John Falzon

Hush by Dominique Hecq

Preparations for Departure by Nathanael O'Reilly

The Tiny Museums by Carolyn Abbs

Chromatic by Paul Munden

The Criminal Re-Register by Ross Gibson

Fingertip of the Tongue

Sarah Rice

Sarah Rice is a Canberra-based art-theory lecturer, visual artist, and writer. She has a PhD in Philosophy and a Graduate Diploma in Visual Art. She is an honorary associate at the Australian National University and has lectured there for many years at the School of Art and Design. She won the inaugural 2014 Ron Pretty poetry award, the 2014 Bruce Dawe poetry prize, co-won the 2013 Writing Ventures International Competition, and 2011 Gwen Harwood poetry prize; and has been shortlisted in numerous national and international awards including the Montreal, Fish, Tom Howard, Yeats, Axel Clark, Michael Thwaites, New Millennium, Jean Cecily Drake-Brockman, C J Dennis, University of Canberra Health, and Philip Bacon poetry prizes. Her limited-edition art-book of poetry *Those Who Travel* (prints by Patsy Payne, Ampersand Duck, 2010) is held in the permanent collection of the National Gallery of Australia and other institutions. Additional publications include the *Global Poetry Anthology, Award Winning Australian Writing, Best Australian Poetry, The House is Not Quiet and the World is Not Calm: Poetry from Canberra, Island, Southerly, The New Guard, Aesthetica, Verity La, ABR*, and *Australian Poetry Journal*.

Sarah Rice
**Fingertip
of the Tongue**

First published in 2017 by
UWA Publishing
Crawley, Western Australia 6009
www.uwap.uwa.edu.au

UWAP is an imprint of UWA Publishing
a division of The University of Western Australia

This book is copyright. Apart from any fair dealing
for the purpose of private study, research, criticism
or review, as permitted under the *Copyright Act 1968*,
no part may be reproduced by any process without
written permission.
Enquiries should be made to the publisher.

Copyright © Sarah Rice 2017
The moral right of the author has been asserted.

National Library of Australia
Cataloguing-in-Publication entry:
Rice, Sarah, author.
Fingertip of the tongue / Sarah Rice.
ISBN: 9781742589527 (paperback)
Australian poetry—21st century.

Designed by Becky Chilcott, Chil3
Typeset in Lyon Text by Lasertype
Printed by Lightning Source

This project has been assisted by the Australian
Government through the Australia Council, its arts
funding and advisory body.

 uwapublishing

For my father Allan Edward Rice (1934–2012)
who made sure poetry was always within reach

Internal compass (for my mother)

When, in my reeling doubt
I turn and turn again
free-wheeling on my axis
hovering, hesitant
My fragile face turned to you
my thin hand raised in question
quivering, wavering
Which way?
The needle-point begins to sway

Leaning, I feel the slow shift
push and pulse
of you, mother-magnet
my motor, my meter
Your spirit-metal
guides my body-earth
Beyond hand
before voice
you whispered north into me.

Contents

Speaking bluntly **13**
Mid-point **15**
Trampolining **16**
ƒishing tackle **18**
Love and dentistry **20**
Things I couldn't say due to laryngitis **22**
Unspoken **25**
Not dead but dreaming **26**
I took a leaf **27**
Absence **28**
Inverse **29**
Indelible **30**
On the bus **31**
The Whipbird **33**
Tide **34**
Reflections **35**
I am shadow **36**
Rupture **40**
Focus **41**

Climbing **43**
The visitation of the King Parrots **45**
A.E.R. **46**
Dad **47**
On winning the *Bruce Dawe* **50**
The door in 4 parts **51**
Last week **52**
Weekly treatment **54**
Govie housing **56**
From the upstairs flat **58**
Finding a simile for the spirit's resilience **59**
Against the grain **62**
From the bus window **64**
Action (bus route 2) **65**
Rescue **67**
Things I blame poetry for **69**
Adder control **71**
Cat lesson #13 **72**
Spirit level **74**

Centre **76**
Exotropia in three movements of the eye **77**
Vitreous syneresis **81**
A recent encounter **83**
The saying and the said **84**
Finding the words **85**
Coogee in two parts **89**
The foot in inches **91**
Breakers **92**
Broken **93**
Bodies **94**
An ode to my body **95**
Scaffolding **97**
Naked lunch **98**
Self-reliance **99**
Retreat **101**
Sing to the tune **104**
Song of gratitude **105**
Wired **107**
A great gaping hole **109**
Piecemeal **110**

The barn and the birds **111**
Times of the spirit from 30,000 ft **112**
To Canberra, I celebrate **114**
Durras **115**
The mathematics of the day **117**
On the importance recently realised of having a cat **118**
Muse **121**
Starting from scratch **123**
For what you took (an ode to parents everywhere) **125**
Brain (some suggestions) **127**
Letter to my brain at 3 am in a plea for sleep **130**
Petition to all brains from the corporate body **133**
Thank you body for the good times **135**
Flinch **137**
Yawn **139**

Acknowledgements **142**

Speaking bluntly

If words had a weave we would feel when our lover spoke
to us in hessian when we needed satin taffeta, and more subtle
vocal fibres, the inflection of cashmere over merino or mohair.
Or perhaps better, if words spoken could be felt like Braille,

a sensitive perception of the digits, under the fingertips, six
dots raised, pin-pricks really but the pattern is all. If the sound
of the letter felt inside the cheek could have its sharpness tested
by tongue and teeth, before the utterance leaked out, before lips parted

company, we could test the word for bitterness, the way we test a grape,
sucking on the sour fruit in the dark fist of the mouth, holding it
against the light to examine its translucence. Clarity and obscurity
are measurements of density, the length of a word's shadow, its resistance

to light, how sure-footed it is in the dark. Sometimes it seems impossible
that speech is spoken by the likes of tongue and lips, those bodily blood-
filled servants to flesh and heart, hatred and dreams. If words were guests
only in the mouth, surely we would send them forth full and warm,

and perhaps they would carry our message with more care. Words stick
in our teeth like peppercorns. We are so very aware of the rough
edges of the apple core against our mouth's sore corner, of the tough
leather bay leaf left in by mistake, or the softness of silken tofu.

Our lips know for certain the thick ceramic mug and the thin porcelain rim.
We are so good at discerning too stale, too salty, too dry, or too hard.
If we could ink up our words like a thumb-print, analyse the friction
ridges, pick up the underlying interface of the epidermis, the better to transmit

signals, the evidence would present not the word itself but its pressure, and through impression – intention, weight. Words put their hands on us and press. Speech leaves its imprint, a smoky graphite smudge with its map of thin white lines where the fine print lies.

Mid-point

Today they shot 8 people
        while I slept

The killing shots were perfect
        it was said

Think   each walked out
                  were carried in

The boxes stacked

Who let the cells know
        as they digested?

Pushing proteins to the gut
The liver silting toxins

Blood mid-point on its round journey

A thought begins to rise
A word shakes itself loose

The next breath gets in line
        Ready to be taken

Trampolining

It was more that the air sucked me up
drew me like a giant breath
as if the sky were bellows
not the power of my knees and feet at all
pushing against the black netting
and springing lithe into the live nothing
I didn't feel it at all
the push and bend
recoil release
no effort of foot-fall at all
as daylight also fell
fell away and behind
and the blackness below me
grew out around me
in an enlarging embrace
I was weather-creator
wind-chaser
cloud-racer
bringer-on of dusk
and night falling
falling away
and every down fuelled my up
and brought about my down
in an easy to and fro
a pendulum a battery
some exercise in Newtonian physics
My body all motion
all pounce
all downbeat

a conductor and baton both
waving music into air
with flailing arms and flying
I was the universe
breathing in and out
and later in bed
in the same pyjamas
my face still red
and my heart
keeping its *scherzo* metronome
eyes now closed
my body still reeled
in the stars.

*f*ishing tackle

words are hooks
for fishing with
and if the barb
is sharp enough
and pointed
you'll catch an ugly
struggling carp
pulled from the dark
heavy and resisting
it'll bend the line
like a bow

or if not barb
then bribe
a tasty morsel
snail or worm
to bait them with
a whole school
will come to you
a flood of slippery
minnows strung
along your line
and you'll catch them all
if you have worms enough
throw them in a bucket
and watch the flapping
layers thicken

ah
but then
there's the fly
a live sapphire faceted
canary on a string
a tiger lily floating
on its own tangled nest
an orchid spray alighting
a rhinestone rainbow lorikeet
a jesus on the water
whirling dervish
feathers flashing emerald
a thought in gold ignited
it is a word a-courting
and it dances on the sea
and tickles fish's fancy
and kisses them
so rainbow trout
come leaping

Love and dentistry

The tongue that goes exploring
    unbidden
to the reddened gum
the ulcerated cheek
the sharp incisor
and hovers there
    probing
A fat fish among the coral
butting against the gummy flank
pushing its flaccid fullness against the pain
Working its wet way among the crevices and craters
    deep sea diver
is more insistent even when the job has been done
and the rotten culprit extracted with sharp instruments
a misshapen, discoloured lump
    to be discarded
More keenly then the tongue returns
again and again
    unrestrained
to explore this sudden cavity
this troubling hole too large for words it seems
a gap that now must be carried around
And the urge is strong to ram the tongue
into its vast vacant-ness
    however clumsily
desperately spilling over the sides
cheek distended
jaw atilt
full-mouthed and mute

And despite the fact that you have not for one second
forgotten the pain and the rot
     you miss it none the less.

Things I couldn't say due to laryngitis

I'm lonely in my little flat with cat on knee
electric throw and heater on and nothing else
but tele and the endless cups of tea

with waiting til the postman comes in fluoro vest
and powered bike with nothing in his hands for me
and nothing can be said

I couldn't call my kitty in when night had come and fallen cold
could only shake the feeding tin and rattle on the metal screen
in the hope to bid him in – no falling third of calling to be had

I mouthed at someone working on his car
he whispered back at me
he's bought a mini crane to hoist the engine in

and painted all the rust away in the empty rib-
cage under-hood and I motioned with my hand
as if to say it all looks good to me

And in the supermarket queue the lady bagging
all my food had asked me how my day had been
and while I waited for the scanning of my soup

spaghetti mandarins I indicated
to my silent throat that sound had seeped away
had left me with a hollow lot

I wanted most to just say *mmmm* or *ahhh* or *yes I see*
for mainly that's what people want
a showing that I'm on their side and right or wrong

is clear with simple tones – a phonetics of the empathetic
the need for concord to be verbalised
A nod or two just won't do I find

Speakers run aground without these humble offerings
and leave a little disappointed as if perhaps their words
had gone unheard

as if the sounds I should have made in response
would operate like the opening of locks – the draw-across of bolts
as proof the word had entered – I could promise them no key

The black and white of writing seemed to suck
out all the grey of saying – all the tonal shifts were gone
and love was somewhere underground and it always took

too long responding to questions with the written word
a lag time after they'd moved on
a missing of the beat

And while I scribbled two notebooks' worth of words
of greetings thanks how goes with you? The writing
couldn't get across the great divide of silence

as if we stood on two sides of a canyon
(except of course there was a child who didn't seem to mind
and read me all her one-word books – the one with *Hug*

on every page – and patted me as if to say that nothing
more was needed) – And the dead of course – I felt for them
knew just what it was like to know your moving mouth

is seen through thickened glass
is pale against the fogged-up pane – the pain you can't cross
over

to say the things you want so very much to say

Unspoken

For the way the sea speaks to the sand
And hand speaks along with voice
And alone without voice
For the way mind speaks to body
And the body to the heart
For the way night sings to the morning
And the rock pool whispers to the rock
For the way moss listens to the tree
And the seed listens for the rain
For the way feather speaks to eggshell
And the conversation between one skin and another's
For the way a page waits
For the capacity to feel gratitude
For the way foot greets ground
And the dog's greeting at the door
For the way a dream talks to the waking
For the way thoughts speak to the memory
And memory speaks to the dark
Without drawing breath
And renders it silent.

Not dead but dreaming

The trees won't be eating again now til Spring
        Their tongues have turned yellow
                and the bones show through

They will be hungry before long
        Winter is their lent
                A slow fast

At their feet   leaves and acorns
        currawongs rake up
                a rare feast

Further down worms
        make a meal of things
                tubers grow fat

The trees are tight-lipped
        keep their store of stories
                for a later green retelling

I took a leaf

out of the wood's book
It was yellow and ragged
and so am I

I read its single page
It told me of days in the sun
It told me of the long drop

I took the leaf home
and it showed me
Autumn inside walls

the dance of wind
It talked of the rain-water
we hold in our skins

After days on the table
turned tired and dry
the leaf whispered

Is everything meant to hurt this much?
The spine cracked at my touch
brown flakes fell

left a tiny bare tree
tells of the fall
of the leaf's leaves

Absence

Funny how we read even empty
benches in the park as gathering,
huddled, grouped together.

The metal stairs we used to sit on
are honeycombed in structure, rigid
and unyielding, they hold their hollow

hexagons apart. Once we wove the in-
between, spinning the cobwebbed lines
across the gaps in a crazy railway network

map. Funny how you leave a trace on space.
The silver, flattened grass whispers that
here (not long ago) someone lay.

Inverse

Imagine the poem is not a clay bowl
(with all its desire to hold and contain)

but the empty space within
a cast hollow

like Rachel Whiteread's *House*
a counter-monument

to the bricks and mortar of words
a salute to thin air

Indelible

Certain things don't come out ever.
The blue mould aura in the cracked
ceiling of the bathroom. Bleach,
absence writ large as presence,
in the royal blue tracksuit.

The ring stain on the mattress
of unknown origin, matter, fluid,
lover, that leaves it to be rejected
on the doorstop, even by the Salvos,
despite the knowledge that many
tonight will be sleeping on worse.

Things said to you on the school bus
to which you had no answer.
The discolouration of the bottom lip,
chewed over and over, leaving a tooth-
shaped bite of purple in the flesh.

On the bus

Think that someone had to put up all the signs we see along the highway;
had to come with a truck, lay down cones and blockades, haul unwieldy
metal geometries, and wait for concrete to set in the muddy hole.
It's the same with every fence-post and pole, drain and ditch, and each bit
of bridge we tumble across without a thought. Every wire tightened with a
twist of the spanner and the chapped, red hand beneath the canvas glove.

From the bus window we see the orange
cross moving among the yellow diamonds,
large green rectangles and red octagons.
A geometric exercise in fluorescence,
and the man erased by the incoming dark
always on our tail throughout the journey.

What is it about travelling that turns us
to contemplation? Car after car, tree
after tree. Each different but the same,
or perhaps the same but different.
Our eye notices the slight lightening
or darkening of the sky's blank canvas.

And the grass rolls ever past us, slightly taller, slightly browner, slightly
more dense. And rocky outcrops rise up and sink down, and the whole
landscape heaves like the sea. And there are bare patches where the eye
hunts to find a resting place and affixes instead on the rim of the window,
the curtains, tattooed road, the joins and arrows, lights and markings,
and the uneven shoulder always out of joint with its rough, gravelled edge.

Or times when the eye is drawn to the uncanny feat
of scrub that is growing and losing berries, limbs, leaves, bark,
each second, like a sped-up season; a great spinning wheel
of growth, decay. Growth, decay. And we think long and hard
like the thirsty drinking. And the passing landscape nurtures
the passing thoughts, and is most fertile once out of sight.

The night arrives before we do, and brings a repetition in reflection.
The man in the next seat shifts and rides pillion with me in the window.
Our two worlds pressed together in this one pane with its postage stamp
square of light. Rows of travel-twins cheek to cheek joined
at the elbow, framed by the double curtains. Rows of blue
reading lights strung from tree to tree, threaded through the sky.

These words on the page fly along curb,
and glide over railing, drift through field
and road and gravel, and the white line
swoops and bends and arcs towards us
in its flight, and catches us at heel,
and reels us in, and casts us forward.

The Whipbird

I hadn't realised
didn't believe
that the whipbird
really was
called the whipbird
with its lasso noose
around the note's throat
flung out into the scrub
a lyric flick
caught in the branches
and hooked on the wind's barb
In the undergrowth
where the ticks wait to swell
we pass by along the path
with the whipbird's whip at our heels
and the sea calling us over the dunes.

Tide

I've never really understood the tides
   how at one time
the beach is full of water
and all these rock-pools hold
   whole wet worlds
where seaweed is released
   from its dead clasp
   and is set singing
and all is froth and roaring silver
and the sun is shattered
        into crystal
   The turquoise steeps
through darker and darker shades
in its own blue fullness
and little aquamarine busy-
nesses and industries
trade in transparencies
       and opacities
in an even-handed back and forth
and the brown line climbs higher
and higher on the cliff wall

and then nothing
   empty beach
   dry desert
the holes of buried crabs

Reflections

Daylight on the bus
when the landscape heads the other way
Night, when side by side
you come with you
on the journey
And dusk, when on the window
the resolve of your face
set to the west
is stirred
by the trees rushing through it
and clouds ride in your forehead.

I am shadow

I am shadow
I demarcate
one blade of grass
from its brother

and unite objects
together on the wall
hat-stand couch-
corner pot-plant

I make shape
out of line
and frame form
I follow and lead

I am shadow
black bird
in water
twin in air

I take flights of fancy
that cost nothing
It is nothing for me
to fly over hill or field

Nothing escapes me
not even the highest cloud
I follow the cloud and the ant
at the same time

I am as fast as the sea-eagle
but it takes me all day
to revolve around one tree
The magnet has no hold on me

I am shadow
I change one thing
in light of another
The passing cat

cast crooked by rock
The mast warped by waves
The pen broken
on the book's spine

I am shadow
observant
I pay attention
to detail

A basket is all weave to me
I respect each strand
no thinness
is too thin

My edges take on
what I touch
soft wool
sharp wire

I am honest
I do not lie
I cannot pass over
even the smallest wrinkle

I sleep in eye sockets and jowls
and the space between nose and lip
I am all that shows nostrils exist
I am good with spheres

I mould the roundness of breasts
and the cylinders of fingers
I find a way of secretly
touching other people

I am the perfect partner
I believe in pairs
in coupling
I will never let you go

I am shadow
I take no note of caste or creed
I am the great leveller
cliff cup cow are all one to me

Like a child
I run on ahead
then drag my feet when
it's time to come home

I hide under tables
and will not come out
I overreach myself
find it hard to sit still

I become a star
under many lights
and nap at noon
I play hide and

seek with the sun
and I too
lose myself
in the dark

I am shadow
At any given point
I am holding
half the earth

Rupture

I am starting to sense another world behind
this one; beneath the smell of salmon croquettes,
sunlight, and voices filling the train carriage;
behind the familiar scene of people moving
in the grey, railway forecourt. If one looks
quickly, or sideways out of the eye's corner,
sudden the awareness, presence of those other
thousands, hidden in the before, or beyond,
moving darkly in the in-between, shadows
seldom seen; the peoples of Tokyo or Toronto,
a glimpse barely caught, but disturbing for all that,
the smooth surface of the world briefly folding
in on itself; a moment of Mobius mobility.
All moving. My god, so many. In this pressing

together of the present, somewhere right now,
hundreds of kites flock the sky, hundreds of cranes,
metalled and feathered; sun and thunder share
the expanded scope, star and torrent and silver.
Dawn and dark overlaid. Somewhere in the whisper
of this stringy casuarina out the window, is heard
the bellow of red oak, row upon row in California,
the dark acres of pine, the sullen silence of moor or
lake or icefield. And under the worn, yellowed carpet
of grasses in Grafton, is a dusty ochre that elsewhere
shows itself as black clod, or Nordic slate. And the sand
blows in from all directions, from a sea that tears at the land's
seams. Far too big for any one moment to hold or with-
hold, to stand or withstand. So many, so much, so long.

Focus

Once you start spotting sad people
   you can't stop
   lonely people too
or people who look like they are being slowly
   pressed inwards by some force we can't see
or children with adult problems
People whose day has maintained
   the left over taste and smell of the week
or people with rounded shoulders
   and hardened spirits
or whose shoes tell a sad story
Those who carry a bag of white bread rolls
   loose and stale
Or those who walk a bit too slowly
   or who look around
   or down
   or not at all
whose eyes have actually, silently
   rolled inwards to traverse a hidden landscape
People who nibble at their lip
or whose face was set over a fight in the morning
   with someone growing ever harder to love
   and hasn't unfolded yet
Those who go about their tasks
   having forgotten who they are
   knowing only what they are doing
   or what they must do

Or those who remember only
   what they did
   or didn't do
People who sit a moment longer in the car
   with hands still on the steering wheel
   once they have parked
   before getting out
People on the bus whose bag occupies the seat next to them
   their silent companion
Or people whose inner wire is pulled taut
   or hangs slack
Those whose problems you can see
   and those whose problems you can't see
People who talk too much
   or too little
   or not at all
who can't find words, or family, or lovers,
   or themselves
People with a small stone in their shoe
   and whose path is narrow, or long, or hard,
and ever uphill.

Climbing

Life, like climbing, is best
accomplished if you don't look
down. Pressed up against the rock,

rock-face to face, one is safest.
Hands like to be busy, little nest-
builders, hunting for hand-

holds in the crevices and creases,
they work best in the dark,
by feel; creatures of tactility.

Feet too, like to work unhindered
by the head; plodders, doers, dour
followers of simple commands, the

dogs of the body; 'come' 'go' 'stay'.
The toes curl instinctually, toe and
ledge communicate directly. Spread-

eagled thus, we are strangely calm,
a flayed skin, stretched and pinned
at our four corners. Each hold hard

won, each inch fought for. Our centre
magically transported as each point
moves, tacked and re-tacked.

Always look the grey granite in the eye,
stare it down to its components, to bits
of black quartz and white quartz, to its

mineral heart. Look to the basest element.

The visitation of the King Parrots

in the Jacaranda tree
above the two women
digging in the sun
in their swimmers

making garden beds together
   re-laying each heavy stone
as a border to stop the grass advancing

Though no stone will be heavy enough
   even between them
to halt the spread of that malignancy
that has already taken root
   inside the one.

A.E.R.

(After Hannah Bertram *I found you in the Garden. Someone left you there*, 2008, twelve glass panes with decorations etched into dirt and moss)

We left you there with an orange
pillow under your head and the morphine
phial still in your abdomen, and drove
away with your clod-hoppers in a plastic bag.

We'd taken you in there and somehow
it seemed wrong never to bring you back.
Twelve long weeks were etched into you.
Time became transparent. You become opaque.

I look for you in the pots and pans, in your silver-
strapped watch. I don't find you in the glass-
y-eyed photographs, or in the jar of dust.
I find you now in the Garden.

Dad

We would sit on the wings of his knees
and see-saw our way through stories
        magical suitcases
                Romanian folktales
        golden apples
              and sea voyages
Sister   and I
        bookended
        holding each square corner
        and turning the pages

Sometimes it was pontoon
betting with matchsticks and forgetting
to hold the plastic cards out of sight
in our keen bending over the game

The tooth-cleaning song
upstairs and downstairs
and always ending with *pie*

Gathering leaves into high dry piles
        with crinkly edges
            in a navy roller-neck
Planting out and potting up
with rubber knee pads over the jeans
engaged in a small prayer service
to the row of terracotta pots laid out on the grass
and after offering fistfuls of potting mix to each

his large palms open on his knees
showed the black grains clinging along the creases

Unwrapping fish and chips from layers of grey grease paper
        that the oil had already worked through
Singing Irish shanties
        Scottish ditties
                gold rush songs in the car
and walking hand-in-hand across the car-park

     Playing squash together
the two of us in that odd white square
with old wooden rackets and older dunlops
the long reach of his hand letting him sit pretty in the centre
while I wove crazily about him in a mad maypole dance
      of sweat and the rubber slap of shoe-soles
with the tiny ball greying but warming over time
til it was a hot coal burning in the palm each time it was retrieved

Still the love of paprika and garam masala
     dukkah and kimchi
         fennel seed
     curry powder
         turmeric
biting on the bitter seeds and smiling
palmfuls flung into the pan with abandon
and the remaining powder clapped away in proud applause

And a very cold night in a tent to see Halley's comet
      which I never saw
but swore I did with nods and *ahs*
when he pointed and held the binoculars for me
      despite the fog-smudged sky
and over-night involved a mid-sleep trip
to the concrete toilet-block together in the blackness
and an impromptu run around the cold field
to warm ourselves in the strange emptiness

      And parties where
           after egg and spoon
the orange wheelbarrow was filled with more than sister and me
      more even than all our small friends put together
           We would clasp the plastic rim
and it would buckle and tilt on a crazy angle
but he always got the big wheel turning
      could always lift us
push us round the garden
no matter how many
how heavy.

On winning the *Bruce Dawe*

Dad this prize
is really yours

For the reading on knee
and quoting at table

and that ineffable glow
on your face

(not just the wine)
when your mouth was full of poetry

For the way you touched books
flipped them open on your palm-wide hand

as if to drink from them
and the way you knew where each one lived

as if visiting friends
knowing who's in no. 3 or 10

as if you were merely dropping
round for tea

You too had *Sometimes Gladness*
and you passed it on to me

a lot more often than that

The door in 4 parts

    1. The glass door   frames the day
        invites it in   but keeps it on the step

This one has pink blossoms in it   like fish in an aquarium

    2. Light comes in-   to its own
    through a crack   Runs its blade
    to prise it open   reaches in
    with long   white arms

    3. Hinges   There's something vital
    about *ajar*   as in   Leave
    the door ajar   An invitation
A reluctance to depart   Willingness to take part in
    what's happening   elsewhere

So that while you're cracking   walnuts
    you still hear the poem   being read

    Still taste the wine   at the other table

And while the ins and outs of   conversation slide
The laughter comes through   like a bell

    4. The door closing   As a child
after we'd been put to bed   sent sailing off to sleep
Dad would give two tiny taps   from the outside of the door

    goodnight love   he'd whisper through the frame

And I swear those words   would still be there
along with rising height-lines   texta'd in the frame

    I'd give a lot to hear   those little taps again

Last week

a grab-bag, lucky dip of trinkets

Monday
an almost date
not quite there yet
hair short and key chain
a sensibility with no suitable

with an almost boy
still high voiced
dangling
pronoun

Tuesday
an altercation
with me the ham
in the measured distance
they wear between them
It would be easier with string
where they could circle each other

between my neighbours
a matter of 2.5 metres lost
the courts have deemed
a portable no-man's land
or a bull-ring
keeping one hand on the rail

And *Wednesday* the marking
administering *adalimumab*
the contrast suddenly horrific
The long lance of light
alcohol swab cotton buds
out of air from the steeple
like ink awaiting writing
fillet of gut squeezed by my left hand

of my little act of bravery
by self-injection
of shiny steel and stomach
paraphernalia on the table
the plunger and the pressing
Each tiny drop gathering at the nib
on my cold fat fish trembling
into a ready fold –

Ready

and in that blank line waiting
To push that thing in there

a whole world of doubt and reticence
Not sure I could go through with it

And then there's the rest –*Thursday*
now he's not in pale pink baby yellow

my father's begonias still blooming
and sunset

Friday the planting out of bulbs
but won't know for weeks to come
I water the bare dirt and hope

Sparaxis I think
have forgotten even where they are
What have they begun to do down there?

Saturday - the empty paddock between

two picket posts

And *Sunday* learning the Requiem
which really is too high for me
from our choir master
who tells us off in no uncertain terms
has almost all but kicked the joy
hobbled the piece at the knees
to the night before now
about two knees

Brahms
and elicits harsh critique
cum school mistress
and calls us strangled cats
out from under our feet
which brings me back – forward
to that feeling of a poem coming
laughing at each other.

Weekly treatment

Tuesday slips again from me
Falls from my week – grip

The tossing starts at midnight
And the sickness comes in like mist

All at sea – pulse bigger than a ship bell tolling
The rolling plank well beyond walking

For my knees have locked onto an idea
And won't give up for quids

The ankles too set in their ways – don't budge an inch
And hands have turned against their nature

Can't seem to grasp the problem
Bottles of pills keep a tight lid on things

And the breath – goes without saying
Won't even – stop – in for a minute

Has to *run* – But methotrexate makes all metaphoric
Everything horizontal – *the bed is made* now lies

For all is 'turning world' with no 'point' still – enough!
– and Eliot even a lost tongue

My body is becoming flotsam – I've put my organs
Up for adoption

Where has my handle on the week gone –
To bring the *carry on*?

Check in – the feel of freshly laundered flannel
Heel of lover's foot in-step

The graphite of the night writing
Its second script and counting

Tintinnabulation of Arvo climbing stairs –
Note well – they do not miss a beat

And last but well – not least
My father's far-off greeting cheating death

And after-all
Tuesday comes around but once a week

Govie housing

Three times at least a week they come around
and look at me   watching them   through the curtains
through the window   through the roses   in my garden
that bear the thickest thorns I could find

They came to take the kids off them first   and then the dogs
two Dobermans   moving in slow motion like a tide coming in
but oh so silent   nose parallel to the ground
an arrow on legs   the bow already pulled taut

It's not just them you know   coiled tight
It's the whole place
You have to watch your washing
for it too has legs and goes walking

It's best to hang the worst sheets outer and the good shirts inner
on the line   hidden to the roving eye
turn all things inside out and peg them roughly by their thumbs
with scarecrow undies at each corner

Every week a new group gathers   by the dumpster
7 DVD recorders   computer screens
Possums breed in all the carports   despite the chicken wire
piss on all my cardboard boxes   they scream at night and thunder
                                      on the roofs

To see a clean shirt   with clipboard   means the housing manager
without clipboard   means court day
Next door has an AVO against the one above
a matching one against them from the other side

who brings me plums and potatoes in a blue bucket with the dirt still on
The one he has to keep 100 paces from lives 10 paces from his door
bakes me chicken tagine when my methotrexate dose has poisoned
half my blood and my bed becomes a wild canoe in white water

Her non-live-in lover   for housing's eyes
helps me dig the big holes   in the garden
in the morning   before the booze has settled in
the wine leading to a heavy hand in pruning

like the time he cut my wormwood tree to the size of a tiny basil
which he hid in a pile of dry leaves   lord knows why
He tapped it with his boot when I asked
where the hell my tree had got to

They'd drunk my wormwood tree
Wormwood makes good booze you see
And one long gone
who I only peeked at

through the spyhole   in the door
and only ever past midnight
when he howled and called my name
to help his drunken legs up the stairs

I never helped him you know.

From the upstairs flat

I can actually hear him peeing
    like a horse
or someone emptying a bucket
from a great height
    above my head
It must go through the pipes
Bathrooms always act as amplifiers

Sometimes it's the only sound
    I hear in the night
Sometimes we do it together
synchronised across the concrete divide
    my ceiling
    his floor
an unpleasant sort of intimacy

    And sometimes
it is a type of private
    language
in the dark
like the tapping
    between two
        prison cells

Finding a simile for the spirit's resilience

Is the human spirit like a bladder
that can only hold so much

leaving us the possibility
of unification through urination

a base commonality
of limits fixed but shared

Or by extension – a loss of elasticity
can with practice be reversed

increasing capacity – tenacity
through a regimen of training

like stretching a calf muscle
each day another increment

akin to the rubber band
theory of IQ

Or switching – is the spirit an open
plain   ploughed plot

a space   a dormancy
awaiting planting

where each of us sows our lot
and the reaping depends on soil or seed

or the temperament of temperature
and weathering the weather

Or is spirit the growing thing itself
the sapling say that reaches

round the navy shade
to find its slice

of light and rushes
to fill the welcome gap

the way air takes up
the volume that's allotted it

always plays squatter
the way a hermit crab moves

from larger to larger shell
as it outgrows its old abode

Or in this rushing to fill space
is spirit more like water

the way with ever more
volume and momentum

water grows its own place
enlarges its enclosure

creating deep craters
carved in the earth's crust

Or instead is it the land
withstanding the sea

shoring up its sand-bagged banks
against the rising tide

Is it the root that catches
firm against the river's clutch

Or is it the floating leaf
letting go in the free flow

Or is spirit finally knowing
when to be the wave

the root the sand the shore
the space the soil the seed

When to push at the limit
and when to accede?

Against the grain

Many things have a grain best not to go against
Even slicing ginger we come across it
   the fibrous root close enough in this way
   to its woody neighbour oak or pine
An anchovy can be slid along the tongue
   only in one direction
   without the salty bristles catching
A dog, a fish, a man's cheek
   and most materials have a grain
   velvet, suede
Some grasses cut the palm
   when their long thin blades
   are drawn the wrong way against it
The quiet perfection of a feather
   is ruined with reverse of stroke
   and never returns
The large headed bloom of protea
   is all pink velour one way
   and ruffled galah the other
Friendships too have a grain
People in general
Ourselves in particular
Time itself is a grain we cannot go against
   even if we wanted to
The morning light slicing cleanly through the dark
   the shadow as it climbs the hill
There is only one way to move
   through a night thick with thought
   and thin on sleep

You must keep going onward
There is no way to crawl back up
    the funnelled pitcher plant
its hairy follicles draw us deeper into the rosy throat.

From the bus window

The trees are fastest
      passing
in their grey dash
backwards

then the middle
      distance
usually a field or lake
disappearing

and slowest of all
      is the blue
mountain range
overseeing all

And I thought
yes   it is right
this equivalence
of pace and decay

But it is we
      me
us on the bus
who pass fastest of all

Action (bus route 2)

There's someone living in my bus
                                      stop
two bikes three bags and a pair of
                                      crutches

He's been there three days now in the round concrete shelter
with the blue and orange *Action* logo and the submarine windows
where the wind whips
                            round and about

There's a curved plastic seat in matching orange
                                   and on it a guy
although today he was lying under the nearby oak
        in amongst the roots of it
                his feet in the dust
and his shoulders pressed into the ribbed bark

I'm not quite sure what to do
But each time I've gone to the IGA
I've bent my steps to pass his little home
                                  and wondered

                I do after all have a spare room
but by spare I mean it has all the things I can't seem to spare
        that sit round me like children – stuff and stuff
with flaccid faces and plump bodies – bags
of books from the Life-line book-fair

       which gave me just last weekend
the feeling that all was right with the world
                so many there – all reading

all scurrying and burrowing between the covers
taking fistfuls of spines
grabbing and thrusting at the tables
all B104 and European History and Card Games
remainders and collectables and tables long and stretched

and the dust floated upward like little spirits
and a musty mould clung to many

But now that all seems somehow cheap
– a bit trashy novel at the airport as you wing your way in from Hawaii
or return from that business thing in Ontario
              with little matching wheelie bags

        and the transatlantic annoyance lasting longer than the jet-lag
that the earphones on the inflight entertainment iPad
gave only a right sided take on things

And those green Coles bags in my spare room
with all their worlds of paper and philosophy
sheepish counterparts to those down the road
        sitting squarely on the orange curve
spilling their helmet jeans and t-shirt secrets

and the crutches lean against the bikes
        and the man leans against the tree

              still

Rescue

We're saved over and over
by the sun on a horse's back
thin white bow shot like an arrow

to be caught by my eye in the bus window
Poetry is therapy if and only if
food and rest are therapy

and a long talk with a good friend
Or holidays and swimming in warm water
and seeing beautiful things

are all also called therapy
We're saved every day by the lime-green
look of wattle in the morning

freshly laundered flannel
Or a lake turned to a field of grass
By getting to the good part in a novel

And by making it home just in time
for your favourite show
Finding the last of the winter boots

on sale are in your size
Hearing that the ewe who tried to birth
all night in the cold on her own

straining on the frozen ground
had twins who lived
licked on their knees in the frost

Watching the weekly growth
of a child you know very well
using her words her fork her hands

holding the watering can
speaking her mind
Watching a cat watching you

in the dark
all detached eyes
And to feel truly understood

in your darker moments
To suddenly get the point
the joke the meaning

A poem throws out life   lines
the way life throws out life lines.

Things I blame poetry for

The inability to watch a sunset
without commenting

to make love
without naming

No longer knowing which is sweeter
the cherry or the feel of the word in my mouth

A dissatisfaction with the skin of things
wanting always the flesh and the skeleton

Having an all too lewd view of fruit
and a hitherto unheard of love of spotted gum
                    porcelain
                    fairy wren
                    spinifex
                    parallax
                    wood pile stacks

An unhalted tendency to list things
and an unhealthy taste for the Latinate

A habit of noting the habitual
the instinctual and the banal

A surreptitious and shameful interest
in sorrow borrowed from next door

Seeing the oak's magnificence and its demise
in the acorn

The inability to block out the sound
of the world's barely audible hum

Knowing the way the moon feels
when the pallid morning comes

The understanding only lately perceived
that poetry demands blood for its ransom.

Adder control

There must be a reason I've met more snakes in poems
than in person

There seems to be something about the sympathetic system
that needs to keep testing the alarm

And no better place to stumble on one
than in the middle of a line

An enforced caesura in the poem's backyard
when the moving hand was heading somewhere else entirely

Reaching say for a word – a *hoe* – a *hose*
The *horse* is startled   Up it rears   Off you're thrown

A poem is the safest place for snakes
(and unrequited love   and death)

What straight-forward mastery to turn a snake aside
with a single word

To kill it with a key-strike
begone

By the time you've got a *rake* in hand
The snake is dead

Its tiny diamond head
a pointed full stop

Cat lesson #13

You know, of all the things I've caught
    my cat doing
I've never caught him
    worrying
in the night

I know this because
   each time I lean forward
into the grainy grey hours
   with pjs grasping my torso
in a twisted knot

    my back a cold gateway
to shoulders unpleasantly exposed
and my legs hot with the heavy heap
of coverings and the weight of midnight
    pressing down

I look over the doona hills and there he is
    in the bedding valley
a tight ball
    tail over nose
his front paws bent

    in I would say prayer
except for the fact it's so clearly not
nothing more than a wheel of warmth
although sometimes he purrs in his sleep
    or tucks his head in deeper

There he lies – a black full stop
to my every unending question
      a full stop as if to say
(that I am slowly learning to read as)
enough now

sleep
   And this labour too
he brings to a quiet circle
   of conclusion

Oh my still point

Spirit level

The level of my spirit has slid
                slightly to the left

My air bubble tilts
                in the blue sea rectangle
missing its strong vertical
                by say half an inch

That clear moving eye winks
                at me from its window

The round empty face pressed
                up against the glass
never lets on
                it's trapped in there

Funny how the spirit rises
                when you drop your end

An easy measure of optimism

They say a flute without a hole
                makes no music
and the hollow in this channel
                allows for the movement

Is a bubble a thing
                or a no thing?

What then is this nothing in the spirit
        that offers movement
                balance
                          rising optimism?

That marks how far off-
                centre we've fallen?
The slide-rule that governs
           our slippery slope

The silent eye that watches
           how we incline

                  and decline.

Centre

The centre of me moves

                Today for instance
it is that hollow place beneath the ears
where the gland dwells in its jaw cave
Sometimes it is the drumming gut
Sometimes breath
                    or a woman
and sometimes
that dark cavern under the ribcage
of Rembrandt's Anatomy Lesson
                horribly emptied

              At least
these are all the places
at which I can be undone.

Exotropia in three movements of the eye

Strabismus

	My left eye takes its job
seriously	stays right
	out
left	as in cricket when sent out-
	fielding into un-mown grass
	Apparently it's peripheral
scanning	Lord knows what it's looking
out for	It's not interested in
central things	won't focus on books or faces
	Not a black-letter
	fellow
	but way out there
type	It doesn't often report
back	But sometimes when I give it
leave	It tells me of a red balloon
	or the smile on a
passing	dog

Nystagmus
My eyes switch
          from right to left
neither spot on
          target
Back and forth
          one becomes two
a false diplopia
          the second image
fixed in air
          where it is not
a form of creation
          which shows more
than anything
          the capacity
of the brain
          to conjure

Is perhaps the origin
          of belief in ghosts

Diplopia

    My optometrist said

                  that eye disorders

    match personalities

    The inward turned

                  introvert

    Staring down their own

                  nose

    The short-sighted

                  the world outside

    their own sphere

                  not quite real

    The Impressionists   Monet say
                                     or Mary Cassatt

    interested in time

                  and space

    not so focused

                  on the detail

    Those who always   look
                                     over their shoulder

    And me   gold digger
                                     of life

    scans like a

                  mine-sweeper

and in my unashamed

                      greed
                      for more living

has made a double

                      of the world

Vitreous syneresis

I see you sometimes
as retinal persistence
residual activity
of the nerve cells

You float before me
kaleidoscopically

In sensory perception
you are *positive afterimage*
from where I sit
not so positive

Less solar flare
more dark side
of the eye's moon
dead blood black spot

You are my eye floater fading
not fast enough for my liking
green still around the edges

Like the slow dissipation of sound
from a vibrating string
once the final chord has been struck

After-glow only occurs in the dark
present trace of the recently absent
a haunting in the blackness

I fix my eye on you
trace your tracking
left to right
right to left
and forget
I dragged you here
on the hook
of my eye's trajectory.

A recent encounter

It was how your eyes narrowed
and fired forward
as you yourself leaned backward
Your words while quiet
had such a velocity of hatred
they flew to me like hawks
like black crows
and plucked out the eyes of my heart
like a great soft white potato.

The saying and the said

Timing and manner my mum would always say
and it's true, the how and when override the what
of what's said, and the same is true of poetry.

I don't think people remember their tone when speaking –
other people's yes, but not their own. Tone, like texture, is crucial
for the feel of things – is it honey or cactus, metal or water?

And if the words float toward you like ducks on a pond
looking for crumbs, or if they are the hard grit
embedded in a harsh wind as it lashes your face,

the words themselves matter less than the manner of their coming –
words that slip in to visit you in their night gown, or words that slip
their owner's leash and attack in packs and will not be called back.

Some words have tiny green tendrils that climb like pea shoots,
while others bite their nails and yours. It is a shame we cannot feel
the weight and warmth or will of saying, instead of what's said.

Finding the words

There is perhaps a god
   in words
hiding not in their text
   but their texture

The way butter on hot toast
   sinks in
soaked up by pores

The way a woollen jumper
   scratching
like a hair shirt

requires a softer
   something
   under

The way light falls
   easily
through well-ground glass

but unpolished is opaque
The way washed hair wants
   to be touched

There is perhaps a god
   in words
hiding not in the sense
   but the sensation

    Residing in the pink
tongue with its yellow lichen
    or in the vocal folds

kneeling in the throat
with their narrow hands
    pressed together

or perhaps in the divine
    bellow-puller
mechanism of air

the stream on which words
float – or swim or drown
    or flounder

Or perhaps in the resounding
    chamber
the great cathedral of neck

    and palate cavity
with its sinus flying
    buttresses

Or perhaps the hidden
    music of words
the nasal sing-song

   rise and fall
the sliding register inflections
   the bell or boom

or perhaps in the sharpness
of teeth that cut
   each word

from the endless stream
giving them beginning
   and end

making them bite-
size for the ears
   to hold

or perhaps in the lips
that kiss a word into shape
make love to syllables

or perhaps most likely
   in the warmth
so often forgotten

that each word spills
out on its own body-
heated pocket of air

like a velvet cushion
That if you could catch
   each word

as it passed to another
you would find
   it would still be
        warm.

Coogee in two parts

1. I think of all the people current-
ly with their feet in ocean
linked by sea

as if all uniting in a common
act of prayer
the praying of feet
on wet sand

one – female middle-aged
all in turquoise –
can't help laughing
as the sea encircles her legs
and the next white cascade
threatens to engulf her cuffs

Another – mid twenties
creeps up to the sea
perhaps in deference
to its greater force –
mighty miraculous
stranglehold thing

and the wide world suddenly
becomes smaller
with its circumference ring
of foot-submerged standers
almost like holding hands

and I am one

2. The waves as they come closer
toward me on the beach
show me their dark
green throats saliva-
rimmed and frothing
at the mouth

I stand with my shadow
stretching into the sea
and the languages
of all the peoples of the world
reaching up out of it

as if the waves had deposited
speech instead of shells
onto the sand.

The foot in inches

It's no easy thing
to persuade a foot

It doesn't listen to reason
but some deeper impulse
more like gravity
or the compass
Feet are lead
but lead that leads
more than the magnet
does the iron

Feet are forward thinkers
They are as the crow flies
Feet have moments
of quiet reflection
but feel it unnecessary
to reveal their findings

Feet pick up
something of the slow
drift of continents

They know which way
the tide is flowing.

Breakers

Each wave
before it falls
      in a white-wash
      of its own decay
aims
I think
to make it   whole
      to shore

not one
ever does

Broken

The heart is really
   just like an ankle
Once it has been twisted
   strained
   gone-over
it never has quite the same 'give'

The thickening scar tissue
leaves a tender tentativeness
   and a certain rigidity

Both, with damage
   swell in the night

Luckily we can always
favour the other ankle.

Bodies

Strange the changes that occur
when you no longer love
the one you loved.
Their body shifts back
to a body with its bits
of skin that are pale
bits that have hair
their feet
and underpants
which are faded
and the elastic too tight
or too loose
and the sock line
biting into the ankle.
And you won't be able to remember
that panicked longing to reach out
and touch them.

An ode to my body

You are my unfinished
          extension
exposed to rain
marking off with string
my ragged periphery

You are concrete
        poured brown
but unlevelled
setting white
   and out of whack

You are my workman's
       port-a-loo
   temporary lean-to
that marks how long
this whole thing takes

You are my window frames
        my worldly view
leaned against the wall
You are my rib-cage studs
where the stud-finder thuds

You are uncut sheets of plasterboard
the grey paper skin wherein
       the crumbling chalk
   which cracks and falls
when the skin's pulled back

You are screws still to be tightened
    and doors waiting to be hung
You are my sparky who hasn't come
to wire me up – lay down invisible veins
    to bring the blood-light throbbing

You are my undug plumbing
pipes lying like picked bones on the open mud
You are wind whistling through gaps
and plastic sheets to seal the holes
    and weather in my empty halls

You're not-quite-there-yet
    incomplete
the dangling bits
    the mess
debris

You are the no colour of raw material
with flashes of fluoro for warning signs
and   Do Not Cross
    wear hard hats
and steel-capped boots

You are my *DANGER - Construction Site*
Foundation in name only
You rest on scaffolding not yet secure
You have been left entirely
    in someone else's hands.

Scaffolding

is a strange
sort of building
it is the very symbol
of a shoulder to cry on
it passes on its stability
          in stages
exoskeleton to a body
          forming
a metal pregnancy
          it lends support
is first to every disaster
I wonder if somewhere
          secretly it hopes
one day it will house
          its own family

Naked lunch

There's a peculiar sense of loneliness
that comes of eating – a pie or pastie
in particular in public – or anything
from a paper bag – with grease stains

It's the same with sitting on benches
at the shopping centre on a Sunday afternoon
after the cafes are closed – or buying certain
items from the supermarket – like blister relief

bandaids or sandals from the chemist – carrying a new
bin home on the bus – value packs of undies from woolies
or that fluffy non-slip mat with its obscene cut curve that kneels
at the feet of the toilet bowl – man-size tissues, antacid or anti-

dandruff shampoo – anklet stockings in beige or nude –
We are rendered naked by these little necessities
and obscenities of the body in which we are oddly
alone in our uniformity.

Self-reliance

No one is going to come and save you.
And because of this you must fold
your clothes at day's end

despite the urge to abandon them
to the backs of chairs. You must shake
the crumple of sleep from the sheet.

You must clean your teeth. Wash the teaspoons.
Fold your pyjamas too and lay the neat squares
to rest under your pillow of a morning

despite the fact that in a few hours all
will be done again in reverse. All will be undone.
And there will be no-one to see.

No one will know the bed corners were tucked
into triangles. No one will see the sleeves cross
empty arms against flattened chests and wait quietly.

No one will know if the spoon was licked before it re-
entered the jam jar. And no one will call you to bed
and to the relief of sleep. That midnight hour must be

crossed alone.

The curtains drawn and redrawn, drawn and erased.
Be wary of sitting too long in a warm place, of holding
cups of tea for too long, or lying in bed thinking in the morning.

Be up and doing, up and at 'em. Be the bird
that gets the worm before it eats the apple.
Try to resist writing poetry.

Retreat

I've been here before
   by the mint bush
   and the dry terracotta pots

with the weather-worn table
   a canvas for shadows
and the nails slowly sinking

   into the decking boards
til you can't see them at all
   in their tiny grave holes

The first time I wrote 'joy
   to wake in hut on hill'
but trip two and three

   are sadder
The sun is just as strong
the food is just as good

   and poetry still heals
but my eye alights
   on different things

On the dog bowl empty metal
   that used to be a saucepan
On leaf litter utterly meaningless

twigs and dirt and old grey leaves
    in need only of sweeping up
The way they catch in cracks

and around the foot of pots
    is nothing but annoying
The broom's square head

  no use at all
and so they stay in little mounds
    a second ring of shadow

There is something sadder still
about the inside of a garden pot
    not meant to be seen

The glaze only token-rings the top
    and unevenly at that
The naked terracotta below

  bears its clay cellulite
and texta price tags
    crossed out black

Winter leaves its wake in pots
yellowed things die in them
    unremembered

waiting to be pulled up
   all-limbed in Spring
still clutching their death mound

to make way for a bright new Petunia
Why am I not looking at the view?
I've asked myself this

   for two days in a row
It is there as it was before
   and somewhere I can hear

the wattle beat its yellow drum

Sing to the tune

At any given moment we can be tuned
like a great harp to feel the vibration
of the sound of the creek that marks the east
corner, or the train track behind home.

We can be taught to feel the difference
(with our feet mind you) of arable pastureland
or drought struck ground. Tuned to the passing of low
flying geese, the voice of our child in the night,

or the sound of a hungry calf. To the weather,
the elements, or the earth's compass. The thinness
of the air, the forecasting of clouds. We can be tuned
to other things too. The slow growing disease

under our skin. The lean of our heart. The worry set
fast in our jaw. Tuned still to words from the past.
To old hurts and older fears, or tuned to a shared
secret hidden in a crowded room. Signs of age

in another. The particular noise a possum makes
when it has got in to the garbage. We can be tuned to
hear the subtle inflection of disdain or dislike. Tuned
to the misfiring machine, the missing tooth in the cog

turning, to the sound of a spanner in the works.
At any point we can be tuned in innumerable ways.
At every moment the earth is heard uniquely. Each
string is set singing, unlocked by an unknown key.

Song of gratitude
(after CMAG Canberra Stories Gallery)

For the soft-handled horse-mane hair
of the half moon brush
The gleam of pewter, copper, glass.

For the carpet palimpsest of patterned lives
that lie layered in the deep pile – embedded
wine, coffee, blood, bread, skin, and ash.

For the possibility of preserving presence
and particularity in a photograph.

For the quiet reliability of maps that level
mountains, baptise stream and river
and christen streets. That make a flat
geometry of tower, plaza, town.
And tell you where you are
and where you are not
and where you are going
and how to get there.
That folds the city into squares.

For the iron will of the anvil
and other like instruments
that stay as they are and should be.

For tubes of paint and the infinite spectrum
that gives us sun yellow, yolk yellow
soft and safety yellow, sweet or sour and so on.

For luck on three legs, level tripod,
held steady so it doesn't run out,
with a knowledge the maker of stools
has over the maker of chairs.

For words, spoken, thought, written, read,
unsaid, drawn, erased.
For the silent letter, mute but needed
like the animating principle
that leaves the body lighter at death,
and is the weight of our final breath
The weight of silence lifted.

Wired
(after Rachel Bowak *Duty Cycle Series*, 2006, Welded Stainless Steel)

Have you ever lost weight
counted not in kilograms
or happy inches off the waist
a belt notch or dress size
    but measured in impact

You seem to have lost
    some of your solidity

You're not quite as 3D
    as you thought you were
You slide through your days now
as an envelope slides into the mailbox
the way light slips under a door

You feel sort of hollow
a person in outline only
You lack substance
even the cat looks right through you
    You are all edge-y

Your contents are border-line
the coffee cup the printer
your shoes for instance define your limits
and more because they touch you
    than you touch them

Your pants seem to be wearing
   you like a coat hanger
You feel as the last unfinished pages
of your child's colouring book feel
the boring bits unworthy of the texta

not the octopus spaceman or sea monster
but the mopping supermarket guy
the tram lady
or the one holding the lollipop
   at the kid's crossing

you're the dustpan in the scene
   would be grey
you're the street lamp
the shopping trolley
and the leaning broom

you're what's behind the fridge
and out of reach
You have a little shadow left
   and you cling to it
but something's missing

        The inner you
You're whole   inside
The guts of you are gone.

A great gaping hole
(after Sidney Nolan *Deserted Miners' Camp, Queensland*, 1949)

There are ghosts in the ground again
As there always are
These two hold each other
and kiss with black-lined lips

A black-bird triangle falls
into its own white mine

A halo hovers
around the swing set
As if it knows the future
is under erasure

And in the middle of it all
an empty door

Piecemeal

These things I must steel myself against
Old men packing books into boxes
The empty seat between people at the movies
The smell of armpits on cardigans
Ironing on the dining table with a towel underneath
Friends who no longer talk to each other
Bejewelled butterflies or fairies
And cards with 'reach for the stars'
Square brittle toe nails
And plastic bags filled with plastic bags
A choc chip muffin to celebrate something
And unplanted punnets with the white roots
straggling from beneath the blue plastic
Board games with missing pieces
And everything with pieces missing
And everything that is in pieces
And everything that is missing.

The barn and the birds

Do you know the skeletal barn that wastes
away on the corner, thinner each time we drive
down to Bateman's Bay? More of the clouds float
inside its empty belly with each sighting.

Its lumbar limbs clutch at the weather inhabiting
its intestines, riding and writhing in its holy centre.
More of the outside is inside; yellow grasses certainly,
and dirt. And really now it is all exterior, an x-ray

on the corner, a transparency on the horizon.
We all peer at it, into it, look right through it.
Reduced to bone it weathers the seasons.
Miniature echoes of the barn are scattered

on the beach, where the bodies of sea-faring birds
are grounded forever, permanently beached,
the white lace cathedrals of their tiny frames bleached
and breached; the sand sweeping onto them,

over them, seeping into them
like a hundred marauding ants,
faster than vermin or maggots,
a quick dry death. Both these bony

structures, the bird and the barn,
are churches with empty altars, no
heart, no hearth. The world has broken
in and burgled them both.

Times of the spirit from 30,000 ft

This week thin on the ground – But found in the air writing this
while looking down on a white land no one will walk on
though it has depth of field – and furrows of ploughed cloud
with hills of a sort of foam spray – the density of a northern forest

and there is from and towards – where sun and shadow play their games
and time moves about while a horizon-twin denies his brother below
Earlier this morning – the call of sea to feet
to come wet the arches and stand like a heron

The pull of water to submerge – to want to become part of a wave
to feel the molecules on either side of the skin wall talk to each other
recognising like and like – the original call of floating
always a return – rocked in the abdomen of the sea

And seeing a mother with her child on the beach pouring wet sand
on to his thighs and covering the small sturdy limb in liquid gold
and the slow sloughing off made him giggle and shake
He was a tiny mountain – making the lava flow

In the night before now – the faint pressure as my dad
pressed my hand in passing – a greeting from his other world
While reading in my seat – recognising love
on the page of a poem – following her line –

to the garden – the fruit on the table – led even to her
lover's bed – where I watch her hair unloosed
And the sunset now so bright from the right side
of the plane I don't need my reading light in this hovering

oval of watermelon – Are these the sorts of things?
Or are they the space creators – the place holders
like the Chinese proverb – keep a green tree
in the heart and perhaps the singing bird will come

To Canberra, I celebrate

your thinner higher air
   the way it holds up the birds
your lake in two parts
   a minuet and waltz depending on the wind
your embrace of purple hills
   that raise high sails as they ride the horizon
your trees that gather breath
   while I expend it

Durras

It was the day I made it to the end
of the beach, to where the curve
of the sand hid the river inlet
with its yellowed surface and foam-
encrusted edge, planning its short-step
voyage across the sand-strip
to the sea, but stopping short.

It was the day of the oyster-catchers, one pair
on the sleek black rocks, the surf encircling
their pink legs, the others pied, intent
on their harried, head-lowered gait, skimming
over the sand. A day of floating flotsam cormorants
that at first we thought were dolphins
feeding offshore among the waves' tumult.

And on our return with the beach towels flapping their terry-
cloth wings dry in the mighty wind, over the wooden veranda,
it was the day of yellow-tailed cockatoos, three in a tree,
one just the tail visible, but very audible in its ceaseless
sirening, its relentless signalling of its smallness and its hunger,
to the two dark shapes in the nearby branches, alternately
flashing their red-brown eye and yellow cheek to the wind.

It was a day of couch-grass pulling, the tiny coarse hands clinging
to the stones; of mulching, and the making of make-shift obstacles
around the stalks of baby trees to keep off the big he-roos that would lie
upon them otherwise, their great flanks and powerful legs crippling
the bowed branches. And against the grey wall that faces the sun,

a mixture of the hardiest survivors of the summer, geraniums mostly
and pig-face, a floppy apricot-coloured hibiscus and an odd, left-over rose,

remnant from another time and place, from a different day altogether.

The mathematics of the day

To live in the moment is to freeze-
frame each increment of grey
   of the coming morning

Inhabit each slice of lightness   separately
dwelling now in one quarter granite grey
another quarter quartz

It's Zeno's paradox
his arrow suspended
stationary in the air

flightless
          hanging
          over our heads

And if all is well at $\frac{1}{8}$
and if all is well at $\frac{1}{4}$ and so on
then surely all is well

It's in the in-between   we stumble
The point of the arrow
felt only in the movement

          At the arc's end
the morning sky is
three quarters

          powder blue.

On the importance recently realised of having a cat

to fix you

to the present
by a heart-beat
on your lap

a velvet ear
twitching
on your satin wrist

to stitch you
to each second
before it passes

a claw dug in
to the flesh
of the day

live desire now for out
now for in now for ball or
floor for curling leaping eating

And in every act of hiding
in shadow box or bed sheet
there can be no hiding

from the now-ness
which says *you are here
and I am glad*

*you are gone
and I am in the flowers*

Night time

In the dim light I wake
to the silhouetted horizon-
line of the bed's architecture

altered by the sudden
appearance
of your double steeple –

you too are awake
and take it as an opportunity
for some impromptu cleaning

And if the motor of my night-
time worries start to whirr
they are drowned by the tractor

of your guttural contentment
resonating directly into my chest chamber
where your small but pointy paws

seem to find the soft spot
between each rib
the weight of you presses out the worry

and when from tiredness
you fall flat on my face
through which I have learnt the act

of breathing under-fur
and your body shakes with little tremors
come of dancing in the long wet grass

I think I am beginning to share your dreams

Muse

I wonder whether Clio
if she's not too busy
with that unwieldy trio
of Word, Event, Grand Narrative
Beating drum to relentless march of Time
Wiping down the slaughter-bench of History
Sorting victors' voice from victims' voice
retelling, recalling, recounting
If she's not too tired
from spanning and scanning
the Centuries from end to end
juggling the players and powers
of each town and epoch
place and period
Wooed by Kings and Popes
and Peoples with a Capital
her legs spread across the seas and seasons
through spells of plenty and want
recording those great bright clashes of Mankind
the might and fight and spill of it all
When she has folded
the hundred-told stories
into Her-story
will Clio
if I bring her honey-melon
bathe her feet
and sing to her on moonlit nights
or better, offer myself to her
as scribe or record-keeper

will she repay me
with the small story of me
my mother and father
my house
my own brief path
the history of this day
this Tuesday perhaps
or this afternoon
this place
this table – too small, do you think,
for a history?
Oh muse
Oh mystery
Oh mistress
tell me the tale of me
my here and now.

Starting from scratch

When I'm sad
I start from scratch
from where I am
My hand, for instance
lying here
Look at it

It used to be a tiny thing
unopened bud

stroked by my mother
and kissed by my father
held against his cheek
and popped whole into his mouth
a soft white oyster

Clasped around adult pinkies
A flash of joy at its small squeezing
Fleshy fingers marvelled at
the minute nails magical
a row of perfect shells
dug into sand

My hands grew
the knuckles formed
I now stroke one hand
with the other
and feel my mother's touch
following the invisible groove

the gesture traced
again and again
aligning the cells into calm
laying the skin to sleep

Look long enough
and you can see each year passed
pressed in its folds

Touch needs movement
without it wood and stone
are equally mute
Stroke is built into fingertips
sliding back and forth
and in that short journey
the inch traversed
from the thumb's axis
so much is felt.

For what you took (an ode to parents everywhere)

Give it to me! with whispered horror
and a curled lip to the boy (3 perhaps 4)
beside me on the plane

He handed it over – a small off-white thing
that must I thought have been a baby
tooth fallen out

but as he didn't clutch his jaw
or seem at all troubled (more ashamed)
I started to think it must be snot or phlegm

Mothers after all are the keepers of such goo
Or perhaps it was a tiny chewed-
up piece of paper that he had spat

Whatever it was got pressed into her hand
I turned away so as not to see
where she secreted it

And I remembered hearing parents often suck
snot from the nose of newborns
so they can breathe through a heavy cold

It reminded me how parents take all kinds of shit
used tissues soiled all sorts of things
wet trodden leaves already disintegrating

band-aids floating off slimy in the pool
chewing gum spat directly
back into the palm

scabs recently removed
(I kept Christmas-beetles in my lunch-
box with rotten bits for them to eat)

and nasty-tasting half-spewed things
that won't go down and hairbands
with a clutch of tufts and the kidney-

bean still glistening from the tin
proffered forth as toddler gift
to hungry mum and mud-pies

to pretend to munch and lunch
gone off in unpacked school-bags
over holidays

A wonder it is to me how mum or dad
reaches out to such things
accepts all with open hands.

Brain (some suggestions)

Be the shell of a lobster
all red shield and jaw-like claws

Be the sea too – and calm
as on a windless day

Be sand that comes and goes
liking to be carried to new shores

Channel tide suddenly arrived
swirling into gaps

Be the sharp beak of the Angler
who watches   waits   darts

through the surface of things
to catch that unseen gleam

and hooks it live   golden
and writhing

Be the thin lips of a vice
your hardened mouth clamped tight

Be autumnal
sweeping clean away

Be the afternoon stillness of a dam
inviting water life to your living edge

Be the gathering storm
holding conference of cloud

a meeting with winds
of opposing opinions

Be the dark
and the voice in the dark

Be the moon
who is not afraid to step forward

Be the legs of a cricket
who sings in the night

all whirring motion
stirring the air

Be frost that grows   Lord knows how
overnight lace on the lawn

Be old bark shedding
in long pink strips

with new white skin
smooth underneath

Be a bare-rooted fruit tree in winter
an exercise in patience

grey   As yet unknown
a stick in soil

Be the slow-growing bulb
The quick rising dough

The spinning of webs
Or of moss

The laying down of snow
The rising up of mountain

Be the child with a crayon
Learn how to make do

Be the master of heart
Be its servant too.

Letter to my brain at 3 am in a plea for sleep

Thank you brain for your six-lane highway
    that plays half a dozen bars of Bartok
        on repeat refrain all night
while sorting tax receipts
and recalling final words
all the while picturing in some mental corner
    Spring's as yet unseen petticoat-petunias
        purple with white skirts
Thank you for these sleep-time digressions
For the white-wash of vitrine storms that rage
    in your shaken snow dome
For your worm-farm of worry
    pale subterranean work
    that keeps the pink threads long and lean
For you record-keeping and record-making
laying down the tracks needled into flesh-shellac
For your vice-like grip on grief
    we'll never lose them that way
For your endless bovine chewing of day's cud
Thank you brain for your sudden remembrances
    of missed birthdays   medicines   memos
That I had forgotten for instance
    to take this morning's *Leucovorin*
    in a bizarre chain of associative
        hide and seek
For your spree fey wildness run amok
        toss and turn spinning
    during mindfulness meditation

and your determined silent focus
    while planting or painting
For your steadiness in the face of that face-
down guy we found passed out on the pavement
    and your quick capacity to organise a crowd
Thank you for taking the trouble tonight
    to lend all your weight
        to my problems
I can see you're losing sleep over it
Thank you for your manoeuvrability
    around complexity
your yoga-like capacity to stretch and bend
    surgeon's ability to dissect
        stitch and heal
Your runner's instinct for the road
Your need to look back
    over the shoulder
Hoarder's delight in ever more stuff
    Tenacity at the enormity of the task
Your whisper in the ear of the dark
Thank you for your needle keen receptor to pain
        and prickly thoughts
Dog with a bone
Demolition man
You keep lists like a bee-keeper keeps bees
    all buzzing slotted into different boxes
Magician who whisks me away while asleep
    to childhood houses suddenly without staircases
Who introduces me again to the Dead

Some small things I would ask of you
Please listen more closely
      to heart and feet
They have a different intelligence
Try to keep better hours
Please stop involving gut in everything
Try expanding your music playlists
You who notice birdsong and name it   *Lark*
and look for my PAYG slips without leaving the bed
   search each room and drawer with neural hands
With your love of numbers
even now somewhere under everything
                      counting   16   17   18
Be less good at your job
Feel free to let me down
Your dedication to the task
   will be the undoing of us
Loosen your grip
Take your eye off the ball
   Falter in your step
      or we'll fall.

Petition to all brains from the corporate body

We the undersigned appeal
to you collective brains
in your sped up evolution

we propose a dissolution
enact an abolition
offer a supplication

for wound back activity
a renewed proclivity
for less tenacity

more conviviality
a meditative ability
and a new avidity

for forest walks
and mountain hikes
less fractious talk

causing over production
of emotional eruption
sleep disruption

and mood disturbance
We propose the emergence
of a somewhat divergent

philosophy of mind
and seek to remind
that brains should be kind

to the body that houses
the spirit that rouses
and the will that espouses

a raw phenomenology
material biology
non-Cartesian psychology

a hand in hand mentality
for complementarity
an embodied complicity

with more responsibility
responsiveness
repose

re
a real
relationship

we await your response.

Thank you body for the good times
(after David Malouf *Seven Last Words of the Emperor Hadrian*)

1. Climbing fences
in staggered shade
and swinging on the gate
The blood plum's stain
on fingertip and thumb

2.   Falling
asleep cheek by jowl
with arms akimbo
palm to palm

3. And while I loved the racing most
there were the good times in a chair
with wine and cheese or beer and book
the peanuts within easy reach
and something quite baroque to hear

4. Although the parties too were fun
with so and so and et. al.
the times with just the two of us
I'll remember more

5. You and I
we were a pair
The odd couple
You fleshy as a peach
and me, a spirited thing
barely there at all

6. You always had the guts
but I was a prick
of caution, courage, conscience

7. You were tongue
and groove to me
And while I've loved every minute
now you are a grave
                    matter
But I am the last
                    laugh

Flinch

What is it about the backs of knees
        that makes me shudder?
That sinew-bound square
with its surrounding jawbone yawn
that makes it look like an exposed throat
To imagine it slit
            there's the rub
Or the underbelly of the wrist
with its quiet river of veins
       or blue tree roots
and the small round nodes
like stones they wrap around

The pulse is a dangerous thing
hidden beneath like a manta ray
I want to keep my elbows closed
for when they swing open
       like a wide wooden gate
there's too much pressure
           on the hinge
There are other places too
that provoke a sort of horror in me
The bovine back of skull
      bony instep or temple
These are secret places

Dark double to the touchability
    of lips fingers nipple hip
where the body is altogether
        too much itself.

Yawn

Funny how a yawn travels through a room
a pied piper gathering all the rats

In that instant we all draw from the same source
a great swallowed gasp shoved into our lungs

like socks stuffed in a bag
and the long outward sigh

That we try to hide it up our sleeves
makes us culprits in common

like playing truant
with a friend

It's mostly like this
our bodies that bind us together

despite talk of mind's united
mutual goals – a *Weltanschauung*

No, more likely it is that we all pee
bare-footed in the night

with toenails that particular pale shade of shell
and a shadow pressed onto each heel

That at a certain point in the evening
we reel our shoulders in on tiny strings

to catch the small warmth of our elbows
and shrink our silhouette

We all lean the same way as the bus turns a corner
grow a wide-legged stance on a train moving

We all rise
on tip-toe

at the edge
of cold water

And sneezing scares us somewhat
those first few seconds when the breath comes in and in with no end

We know the mundane imperative of bowel
and the incredulity of a broken heart

Our bodies loosen in warmth or water
and we all leave hair on the pillow

We share in the first great O
our mouths make for milk at the start

And the milky grey our eyes
all turn at the end.

Acknowledgments

Many of these poems have been awarded prizes and published in the following anthologies and journals:

A great gaping hole (Shortlisted inaugural Philip Bacon ekphrastic competition as part of the 2015 Queensland Poetry Festival, published *Verity La* 2015.

Absence (Published by The Red Room Company, *The Disappearing* 2012)

Action (bus route 2) (Shortlisted for Michael Thwaites Poetry Prize 2015, published *Capital Letters* ACT Writers Centre)

Adder control (Long listed in the Fish Poetry Prize, 2017)

Against the grain (Co-winner 2011 Gwen Harwood poetry prize, published *Island Magazine* website; and *Long Glances: A Snapshot of new Australian Poetry from the Inaugural Jean Cecily Drake-Brockman Poetry Prize*, ed. Theodore Ell; and *Award Winning Australian Writing 2012*, ed. Adolfo Aranjuez, Melbourne Books, and *The House is Not Quiet and the World is Not Calm: Poetry from Canberra* (eds.) Geoff Page and Kit Kelen, 2015)

An ode to my body (Highly Commended W B Yeats Prize for Australia, 2015)

Bodies (*Best Australian Poems, 2012*, ed. John Tranter, Black Inc. and *fourW twenty-two* anthology, 2011, and *The House is Not Quiet and the World is Not Calm* op. cit.)

Breakers (*Contrappasso Magazine* ed. Theodore Ell, Issue 8, March, 2015)

Broken (*The Canberra Times* 19th April, 2014)

Centre (*Contrappasso Magazine* ed. Theodore Ell, Issue 8, March, 2015)

Climbing (*Australian Book Review online* 'States of Poetry: ACT', 2016)

Dad (*Australian Book Review online* 'States of Poetry: ACT', 2016)

Exotropia in three movements of the eye (*Axon*, forthcoming 2017)

Finding a simile for the spirit's resilience (Shortlisted Fish Poetry Contest, 2017)

Finding the words (Shortlisted ACU Literary Awards, 2014, chapbook publication)

Flinch (Shortlisted Axel Clark Memorial Prize, 2014)

Focus (*The House is Not Quiet and the World is Not Calm: Poetry from Canberra*, op. cit.)

From the upstairs flat (Shortlisted Axel Clark Poetry Prize, 2015)

Govie Housing (3rd place Shoalhaven Literary Awards, 2014, published website, displayed for Gallery of Australian Design (GAD) 'Front Door' project)

I am Shadow (Shortlisted 2014 Tom Howard Poetry Contest; and inaugural 2013 Jean Cecily Drake-Brockman Award, published in *Long Glances: A Snapshot of new Australian Poetry from the Inaugural Jean Cecily Drake-Brockman Poetry Prize*, ed. Theodore Ell, 2013)

Indelible (*Contrappasso Magazine* ed. Theodore Ell, Issue 8, March, 2015)

Last week (Winner 2014 Bruce Dawe Poetry Prize, published website and recording)

Letter to my brain at 3 am in a plea for sleep (finalist *The New Guard* Knightville poetry competition, publication *The New Guard* vol. 5, 2015)

Mid-point (long listed University of Canberra Vice Chancellors International Poetry Prize, 2016, published *Tremble*, 2016 anthology)

Muse (Highly commended 2011 Michael Thwaites Poetry Award, published *ACTWrite*, Vol.18, Issue 3, 2012)

Naked lunch (Displayed in Canberra city for Noted Festival *Bill Poetries*, 2016)

Piecemeal (Inaugural *Metabolism: Australian Poetry Members' Anthology*, 2011)

Reflections (*Southerly* Journal, vol. 70, no. 3, 2011)

Retreat (*Poetry and Place Anthology 2015*, (eds.) Ashley Capes & Brooke Linford)

Rupture (Co-winner Writing Ventures, 2013, publication *Australian Poetry Journal* 4.2, 2014, ed. Michael Sharkey)

Scaffolding (*The Canberra Times*, 30th April 2016)

Self-reliance (*Australian Book Review online* 'States of Poetry: ACT', 2016)

Song of gratitude (Shortlisted Fish Poetry Prize, 2014, published *Australian Book Review online* 'States of Poetry: ACT', 2016)

Speaking bluntly (Winner Ron Pretty poetry prize 2014, published *Australian Poetry Anthology*, vol.4 2015, Award *Winning Australian Writing 2015*, *Best Australian Poems 2015*, *Aesthetica* Anthology 2015 and semi-finalist New Millennium Writing Awards 2015)

Spirit level (*AntiTHESIS* journal, equilibrium, vol.5, 2015)

The saying and the said (*Australian Book Review* 'States of Poetry: ACT', 2016)

Things I couldn't say due to laryngitis (shortlisted University of Canberra Health Poetry Prize, 2016)

Tide (*Australian Poetry Journal 4.1*, ed. Michael Sharkey)

To Canberra, I celebrate (Co-winner *Poetry in Action Award*, poem on ACT buses)

Trampolining (Long listed The University of Canberra Vice Chancellor's International Poetry Prize 2015, published *Underneath*, 2015 anthology, (eds.) Owen Bullock and Niloofar Fanaiyan, Axon Elements)

Unspoken (*The Canberra Times*, 7th March, 2015, used as the Libretto for a choral composition by Philip Batterham, premier performance by Oriana Chorale on April 22nd, 2017 at University House, ANU)

Yawn (Shortlisted Montreal Poetry Prize, 2013, published *2013 Global Poetry Anthology*)

The door in 4 parts (Long listed Fish Poetry Prize, 2015)

The Whipbird (*Island* Magazine vol. 124, Autumn, 2011)

Weekly treatment (Long listed Fish Poetry Prize, 2017)

Wired (Commissioned response to CMAG *Urban/ Suburban* Exhibition, 2015)

www.ingramcontent.com/pod-product-compliance
Lightning Source LLC
Chambersburg PA
CBHW032230080426
42735CB00008B/791